100 AMAZING FACTS ABOUT ITALY

Content

Introduction...8

Fact 1 - Italy in the shape of a boot..............................9

Fact 2 - The Palermo Catacombs................................10

Fact 3 - Vesuvius, the sleeping giant..........................11

Fact 4 - Leonardo da Vinci, Boundless Genius............12

Fact 5 - The Wolves of the Apennines 13

Fact 6 - Pasta, much more than spaghetti 14

Fact 7 - Gladiators, the stars of the Colosseum..........15

Fact 8 - The Strange Mummies of Sicily......................16

Fact 9 - The magical Leaning Tower of Pisa 17

Fact 10 - La Befana, the Witch of Gifts.......................18

Fact 11 - The Invention of Glasses 19

Fact 12 - Marco Polo, Discovering China.....................20

Fact 13 - Sardinian Flamingos 21

Fact 14 - Galileo, father of the thermometer 22

Fact 15 - The Mysterious Gesture of the Horn............23

Fact 16 - Lentils at Midnight, for a Lucky Year............24

Fact 17 - The Mysterious Etruscans of Italy 25

Fact 18 - A Stunning Sistine Ceiling 26

Fact 19 - The Romans and Their Many Gods...............27

Fact 20 - 25 National Parks to Explore.......................28

Fact 21 - Neapolitan pizza, a culinary legend 29

Fact 22 - Caesar, Emperor Like No Other...................30

Fact 23 - The Enchanted Canals of Venice 31

Fact 24 - The Renaissance, a New Golden Age...........................32

Fact 25 - The Hidden Treasures of Pompeii................................33

Fact 26 - Romulus, Remus and a Founding Wolf.........................34

Fact 27 - Roman Tricks for Building Roads 35

Fact 28 - A Venetian Named Casanova..36

Fact 29 - Sorbets and ice creams, thank you Italy!......................37

Fact 30 - Italy's Enigmatic Bermuda Triangle.............................38

Fact 31 - Sardinia, a paradise for wild horses 39

Fact 32 - The Incredible Catacombs of Naples 40

Fact 33 - Pinocchio, a Little Wooden Boy....................................41

Fact 34 - The Traditional Tarantella Dance 42

Fact 35 - Roman Aqueducts, the Art of Water 43

Fact 36 - The magic of Italian Christmas celebrations.................44

Fact 37 - The Invention of the Violin, an Italian Gift....................45

Fact 38 - The Medieval Ball Game "Calcio" 46

Fact 39 - Secrets of the Hanging Gardens of Babylon 47

Fact 40 - The Giants of the Sartiglia Parade................................48

Fact 41 - The Mysteries of the Island of Capri 49

Fact 42 - The Secrets of the Venetian Gondoliers 50

Fact 43 - Italians' love for coffee...51

Fact 44 - The Mystical Cimbri Forest 52

Fact 45 - The Talking Mountains of the Dolomites.......................53

Fact 46 - The Epic of Dante and his Inferno 54

Fact 47 - The Legendary Heroes of Abruzzo 55

Fact 48 - The bright colours of Burano 56

Fact 49 - The Art of Opera at La Scala in Milan 57

Fact 50 - The Mysteries of Lake Como 58

Fact 51 - Stone giants in the Alps 59

Fact 52 - The Mysterious Treasure of Ostia 60

Fact 53 - The Incredible Legend of Rialto 61

Fact 54 - Sicilian Puppets 62

Fact 55 - The Wonderful History of Tiramisu 63

Fact 56 - The Guardian of the Alps, the Ibex 64

Fact 57 - The Explorer Amerigo Vespucci 65

Fact 58 - The Delicious Secret of Risotto 66

Fact 59 - The Magic of the Roman Circus 67

Fact 60 - The Riddle of the Mantuan Labyrinth 68

Fact 61 - The Dance of the Stars in San Lorenzo 69

Fact 62 - The Mystery of Alberobello's Trulli 70

Fact 63 - The melodies of Verdi and Puccini 71

Fact 64 - The Subterranean Wonders of Sardinia 72

Fact 65 - The Fable of King Midas in Sicily 73

Fact 66 - The Secrets of Bolognese Sauce 74

Fact 67 - The Treasures of Hadrian's Villa 75

Fact 68 - Legends of the Blue Caves 76

Fact 69 - The Charm of Roman Villas 77

Fact 70 - The Wolves of Lazio 78

Fact 71 - The Mystery of the Sphinxes of Rome 79

Fact 72 - The Exploits of Hannibal and His Elephants.................80

Fact 73 - The Ballet of Summer Shooting Stars 81

Fact 74 - The Hidden Art of Roman Mosaics 82

Fact 75 - The Poetry of the Fountains of Rome............................83

Fact 76 - The Tale of the Mermaids of Amalfi 84

Fact 77 - The Fascinating History of Limoncello..........................85

Fact 78 - The Miracles of St. Francis of Assisi 86

Fact 79 - The Legends of the Italian Lakes...................................87

Fact 80 - The Delicate Art of Venetian Mosaic.............................88

Fact 81 - The wonderful island of Elba 89

Fact 82 - The Amazing History of Brioche 90

Fact 83 - The fairy tale of the Aosta Valley 91

Fact 84 - The Legend of the Carrara Caves 92

Fact 85 - The magic of the feast of San Gennaro 93

Fact 86 - The dragons of Piedmontese legends...........................94

Fact 87 - The Mystery of the Ghosts of Tuscany..........................95

Fact 88 - The Riddle of the Temples of Sicily................................96

Fact 89 - The Adventures of Saint Nicholas..................................97

Fact 90 - The Mysterious Bridge of Sighs 98

Fact 91 - The Wonderful Valley of the Temples............................99

Fact 92 - Giotto's Art of Frescoes.. 100

Fact 93 - The exploits of the Lombard League............................ 101

Fact 94 - The Charm of Tivoli Gardens 102

Fact 95 - The legend of the castles of the Aosta Valley............ 103

Fact 96 - The Miracles of Monte Sant'Angelo 104

Fact 97 - The Secret History of Panettone................................. 105

Fact 98 - The Magic of Venice's Palaces.................................... 106

Fact 99 - The Fairy Tale of Lake Garda...................................... 107

Fact 100 - The Naval Battles of Lake Bolsena 108

Conclusion... 109

Quiz.. 110

Answers 116

"Italy is a landscape where the past is an integral part of the present."

— Italo Calvino

Introduction

Welcome, dear reader, to a journey through the wonders and mysteries of Italy. This country, known for its cuisine, fashion and art, also holds treasures of stories, legends and anecdotes that many are unaware of. If you're here, it's probably because you're hungry for knowledge, curious to discover the little secrets that hide behind every corner of the Italian boot.

With "100 Amazing Facts About Italy", you'll dive into the heart of these fascinating tales, from the snow-capped peaks of the Alps to the sparkling waters of Sicily. This book will take you on a journey through the centuries, showing you aspects of Italy that you would never have imagined.

Each fact revealed in these pages is an invitation to explore more, to know more and to fall in love, once again, with this country of a thousand facets. You will discover stories of love, wars, miracles, betrayals and discoveries that have marked the Italian cultural landscape.

Prepare to be surprised, moved, and dazzled. Open your eyes and your mind wide, because Italy awaits you with its captivating stories and well-kept secrets. Let's embark on this adventure together!

Marc Dresgui

Fact 1 - Italy in the shape of a boot

Have you ever looked at a map of Europe? If so, you've probably noticed a country that looks like a boot! It's Italy! This country stretches into the Mediterranean Sea and its distinctive shape is recognized all over the world.

The Italian "boot" points south, kicking another island called Sicily. Thanks to this unique shape, Italy has a vast coastline that stretches for thousands of kilometers. This coast has played a vital role in the history of the country, connecting it with other civilizations by sea.

But that's not all! This boot is also very mountainous. The Alps in the north form a kind of "sock" for the boot, and the Apennines cross the country from north to south like a backbone. These mountains have influenced the culture, traditions, and even cuisine of the different regions.

The next time you see a map, think of the Italian boot. It's not just a fun form, it's also a fascinating story of a country rich in tradition and discovery!

Fact 2 - The Palermo Catacombs

You may be familiar with the catacombs of Paris, but have you ever heard of the catacombs of Palermo in Sicily? They are truly amazing and one of a kind!

Let's dive together under the city of Palermo. Here, the catacombs date back to the 16th century and originally served as a burial place for monks. But over time, this practice expanded and many people wanted to be buried there. What for? Because these catacombs had the particularity of preserving the bodies well thanks to a process of mummification.

The walls of the catacombs are adorned with thousands of mummified bodies, dressed in their finest clothes, some of them seeming almost alive despite the centuries that have passed. Among them, the body of a little girl named Rosalia Lombardo, who died in 1920, is one of the best preserved in the world.

The next time you delve into the history of Italy, remember that beneath the bustling streets of Palermo lies a silent but powerful testimony to past life.

Fact 3 - Vesuvius, the sleeping giant

Have you ever heard of a mountain that can wake up by breathing fire? Well, Mount Vesuvius, near Naples in Italy, is one of those mountains! It's an active volcano, but for now, it's dormant... Or at least, we hope so.

In the year 79 A.D., Mount Vesuvius woke up spectacularly. During this eruption, the cities of Pompeii and Herculaneum were completely buried under ash and lava. What is incredible is that these ashes preserved the cities, freezing the daily life of the Romans of the time.

Today, you can visit the ruins of Pompeii and see casts of locals trapped by the eruption. It's a moving reminder of the power of nature. But Vesuvius isn't just a threat; it is also a symbol of the region, visible from almost everywhere in Naples.

The next time you look at an image of Vesuvius, think about all the secrets it keeps. Despite its apparent calm, it is a silent witness to thousands of years of history.

Fact 4 - Leonardo da Vinci, Boundless Genius

When the name Leonardo da Vinci is mentioned, what do you think of? Maybe the mysterious "Mona Lisa" smiling enigmatically at the Louvre? But did you know that Leonardo was much more than just a painter?

Born in 1452 in the small village of Vinci in Italy, Leonardo was a true Renaissance genius. Yes, he was a painter, but he was also an inventor, a scientist, a mathematician and even a musician! His sketchbooks are full of incredible ideas, ranging from flying machines to submarines.

One of his most fascinating projects is the "Codex on the Flight of Birds", where Leonardo studies the movement of birds to understand flight. Thanks to him, mankind began to dream of flying like birds! And while his inventions didn't always come to fruition, they paved the way for many future discoveries.

So, the next time you admire a painting by Leonardo or one of his inventions, remember that he was not just an artist, but an inquisitive mind always on the lookout for knowledge and innovation.

Fact 5 - The Wolves of the Apennines

Have you ever imagined wild wolves sneaking between the trees of the Italian mountains? Well, that's a reality in the Apennines, the mountain range that stretches from the north to the south of Italy.

These majestic mountains are home to many animals, but the Apennine wolf is truly special. Despite the myths and legends surrounding them, these wolves are generally shy and avoid humans. They have a grey-brown coat and bright yellow eyes, blending perfectly into the forests of the Apennines.

For a long time, their numbers declined due to hunting and habitat loss. But thanks to conservation efforts, the wolf population is now increasing. They play a crucial role in the ecosystem by regulating deer and wild boar populations.

The next time you hear about the Apennines, think of these magnificent creatures that silently roam the mountains, preserving a delicate balance in Italy's wilderness.

Fact 6 - Pasta, much more than spaghetti

When you hear the word "Italian pasta", what do you think of? Spaghetti with tomato sauce? But Italy offers a much wider variety of pasta than you might imagine!

The beautiful region of Emilia-Romagna, for example, is famous for its "tagliatelle" and "tortellini". This pasta is often served with a rich meaty or cheese-based sauce. In Sicily, you'll find "cannelloni", tubes of dough stuffed with meat or cheese and covered with sauce.

Further north, in Lombardy, "risotto" is king. Even though it's not pasta per se, it's a rice-based dish that captures the essence of Italian cuisine: simple, delicious, and made with love. Each region of Italy has its own pasta specialties, reflecting its culture and history.

Next time you're enjoying pasta, think about all these amazing types out there. And if you have the opportunity, try to taste as many varieties as possible to really appreciate the richness of Italian cuisine!

Fact 7 - Gladiators, the stars of the Colosseum

Do you realize that Rome, thousands of years ago, had its own superstars? No, they weren't singers or actors, they were gladiators! These fighters were the true heroes of the Colosseum arena.

The Colosseum, Rome's great amphitheater, hosted gladiatorial fights in front of thousands of spectators. These warriors trained hard and mastered the art of fighting. Some were slaves, others were free men seeking glory.

But not all fighting was deadly. Contrary to what one might think, many fights were choreographed or ended without anyone being seriously injured. The goal was to entertain, not kill. Popular gladiators were celebrated as heroes, with fans and sponsors.

Imagine sitting at the Colosseum, feeling the excitement of the crowd, as two gladiators prepare to face each other. It was the ultimate spectacle of the time, a combination of sport, drama and sheer bravery!

Fact 8 - The Strange Mummies of Sicily

Do you remember the previously mentioned Palermo Catacombs? Well, this place still has secrets to let you know! In Palermo, Sicily, you'll find something quite unique: well-preserved mummies looking down at you from the past.

Since the 16th century, catacombs have been used to mummify and display the bodies of monks, nobles, and even some ordinary citizens. Unlike Egypt, where mummies are wrapped, these Sicilian mummies are dressed in their period clothes, offering a fascinating insight into the fashion and culture of yesteryear.

One of the most famous mummies is that of Rosalia Lombardo, a little girl who died in 1920. Thanks to conservation techniques, it seems to be peacefully asleep, nicknamed "The Sleeping Angel" by visitors.

These mummies are not there to frighten, but to offer a silent testimony of the history of Sicily. If you visit Palermo one day, try to stop and meet these witnesses of times gone by, who silently tell their stories through the centuries.

Fact 9 - The magical Leaning Tower of Pisa

Have you ever seen a tower that looks like it's about to fall, but stays up year after year? If you travel to Italy, you'll discover the Leaning Tower of Pisa, an architectural masterpiece that has defied gravity for centuries.

Begun in 1173, the construction of this tower took almost 200 years. Because of the unstable ground, it began to lean shortly after the work began. Instead of abandoning it, engineers and architects adapted their plan, and it became one of Italy's most recognizable icons.

Many people come to Pisa just to take a "fun" photo with the tower, pretending to support it with their hands. But beyond this attraction, the tower is a testament to human ingenuity in the face of challenges.

So, if one day you find yourself in Pisa, don't forget to take a moment to admire this amazing structure. She is living proof that sometimes even "mistakes" can turn into something beautiful and unforgettable!

Fact 10 - La Befana, the Witch of Gifts

You know Santa Claus, don't you? But did you know that Italian children are eagerly awaiting another magical figure during the holiday season? Her name is La Befana, and she is often described as a nice old woman who resembles a witch.

The Befana does not visit the children at Christmas, but rather on the night of January 5, on the eve of the Epiphany. According to legend, the Three Wise Men asked him for directions to find the baby Jesus. After guiding them, she allegedly tried to follow them with gifts for the baby, but was never able to find him. Since then, she has been traveling on her broom every year, handing out gifts to children in the hope of finding Jesus among them.

If you've been good, she'll leave you candy and toys. But if you've been naughty, you might find charcoal (actually, often sweet charcoal) in your sock!

So, when the holidays come in Italy, don't forget to keep an eye out for La Befana. It reminds everyone that the magic of tradition endures through the ages.

Fact 11 - The Invention of Glasses

Can you imagine a world where no one wears glasses to read or see from afar? It's hard to imagine today, isn't it? But there was a time when glasses didn't exist. And guess what? It was in Italy that these precious accessories were invented!

Around the year 1280, in the Venice area, craftsmen began assembling lenses onto frames to help people see more clearly. These early "glasses" were often worn by monks and scholars who needed to improve their eyesight for reading.

Over time, these glasses evolved from simple hand-held frames to devices attached with temples behind the ears. Thanks to these Italian innovations, millions of people around the world can now read, work, and enjoy the beauty that surrounds them.

So, the next time you see someone adjusting their glasses or diving into a good book thanks to them, remember those Italian inventors who changed the way we see the world!

Fact 12 - Marco Polo, Discovering China

Have you ever heard of Marco Polo? This name may just remind you of a pool game, but in reality, Marco Polo was a great Italian explorer who lived in the 13th century. Originally from Venice, he embarked on a journey that would take him to faraway and unknown lands.

During his journey, Marco Polo traveled to the mysterious China, a country far removed from Europe and its culture. He was one of the first Europeans to describe in detail the wonders of the Middle Kingdom, its glittering palaces, bustling markets, and incredible inventions.

For 24 years, he traveled this exotic land, learning its customs and traditions. On his return to Italy, he recorded his adventures in a book that amazed the whole of Europe. Thanks to him, many Europeans discovered the existence of fascinating places such as the Silk Road and the great city of Beijing.

So, next time you're playing "Marco Polo" in the pool, think of that intrepid Italian explorer who paved the way for so many more discoveries!

Fact 13 - Sardinian Flamingos

When we think of Sardinia, we often imagine beautiful beaches and crystal clear blue sea. But did you know that this Italian island is also home to splendid flamingos? Yes, you heard right, flamingos in Europe!

These majestic birds with long legs and pink plumage are mainly found in the salt ponds and lagoons of Sardinia. Their colour comes from their diet rich in carotenoids, small shrimps that give them their special hue.

The best time to see them is between spring and autumn. They settle in colonies and put on an incredible show when they all fly away together, forming a pink dance in the Sardinian sky. It's a real aerial ballet that awaits you!

So, if you have the chance to visit Sardinia one day, don't forget to bring your binoculars. This way you will be able to admire these amazing creatures and understand why Sardinia is so special.

Fact 14 - Galileo, father of the thermometer

Galileo Galilei, whom you probably know as a great astronomer and physicist, had an incredibly curious mind. In addition to his discoveries about the stars and planets, did you know that he played a crucial role in the invention of the thermometer?

In 1593, Galileo created an instrument called a "thermoscope". It was a glass tube containing water and air, connected to a container of water. When the temperature changed, the water would rise or fall in the tube. Even though it wasn't a thermometer like the ones we use today, it was the beginning of a big breakthrough!

It wasn't until later that other scientists added temperature scales to this invention. But without Galileo's genius and his initial thermoscope, who knows how long it would have taken to invent the modern thermometer?

The next time you look at a thermometer for temperature, remember the brilliant Galileo and its innovative spirit. If it weren't for it, we might still be guessing whether it's cold or hot outside!

Fact 15 - The Mysterious Gesture of the Horn

While walking around Italy, you might see people wearing a small pendant in the shape of a horn or even making a strange gesture with their hand, imitating a horn. But where does this symbol come from and why is it so important to Italians?

The "cornicello", or little horn, is an old Italian talisman. For centuries, it has been believed to protect against the "malocchio", i.e. the evil eye. People wear it around their necks or hang it in their homes or cars to ward off negative energies and attract good luck.

The hand gesture, where the small and ring fingers are folded while the other fingers remain extended, is another way to ward off evil. If someone gives you a compliment in Italy, they might do it right after to avoid attracting the evil eye!

So, if you decide to visit Italy one day and you see these symbols or gesture, you will now know that they are there to protect and bring good luck. Isn't that fascinating?

Fact 16 - Lentils at Midnight, for a Lucky Year

Have you ever heard of eating grapes at midnight to celebrate New Year's Eve? In Italy, it's a completely different tradition. There, lentils have a special meaning when it comes to greeting a new year.

Why lentils, you ask? These small, round legumes are associated with prosperity and abundance. Their shape is reminiscent of coins, symbolizing wealth. Tradition has it that the more lentils you eat at midnight on New Year's Eve, the more lucky and wealthy you'll have in the coming year.

The typical dish consists of cooked lentils served with "cotechino" or "zampone", Italian sausages. This meal is supposed to guarantee a year filled with happiness, health, and prosperity.

Next time you're celebrating New Year's Eve in Italy or with Italian friends, don't forget to pour yourself a plate of lentils at midnight. Who knows, this might just be your luckiest year!

Fact 17 - The Mysterious Etruscans of Italy

Long before the power and glory of Rome, another civilization dominated the region we know today as Italy: the Etruscans. These mysterious peoples lived between the Arno River and Rome, a region called Etruria.

Their origins remain a mystery. Unlike other ancient cultures, the Etruscans did not leave detailed texts or epics. However, thanks to their ornately decorated tombs and artifacts, we have clues about their daily lives, beliefs, and art. For example, they had a passion for luxury, as evidenced by their elaborate jewelry and painted vases.

The Romans eventually conquered the Etruscans, but the Etruscan influence endured. Much of what we associate with Roman culture, such as the construction of aqueducts and divination through the entrails of animals, has Etruscan roots.

So, as you walk through today's Tuscany, remember that beneath your feet lie the remains of an ancient and mysterious civilization that has left an indelible mark on Italy's history.

Fact 18 - A Stunning Sistine Ceiling

If there's one place in Rome that will leave you speechless, it's the Sistine Chapel. Located in the heart of Vatican City, this chapel is the jewel of the Italian Renaissance, and its ceiling is probably the most famous masterpiece in the world.

Painted by the legendary Michelangelo between 1508 and 1512, the ceiling tells the story of Genesis in nine panels. Among these panels, one of the most iconic is the "Creation of Adam", where God reaches out to give life to Adam. It's such a powerful image that it's recognized around the world.

But did you know that Michelangelo wasn't particularly keen on this task? He saw himself first and foremost as a sculptor, not a painter. Yet, despite his initial misgivings, he created a body of work that continues to inspire and amaze millions of visitors each year.

So, if you have the chance to visit Rome, don't miss this artistic marvel. Look up and be dazzled by the genius of Michelangelo and the incredible story he painted on this majestic ceiling.

Fact 19 - The Romans and Their Many Gods

Have you ever heard of the countless gods and goddesses of Roman mythology? The ancient Romans had a deity for almost everything, reflecting the complexity and richness of their culture. The Roman pantheon was filled with divine figures influencing every aspect of their daily lives.

Take, for example, Jupiter, the king of the gods, ruler of the sky and lightning, or Venus, goddess of love and beauty. Each deity had its own temple, priests, and rituals. These gods were not just distant figures; They were actively revered, feared, and loved.

But did you know that many of these Roman gods have equivalents in Greek mythology? Mars, the Roman god of war, for example, is the equivalent of Ares in Greece. This transfer of gods shows the influence and adaptability of Roman culture, assimilating and modifying the traditions of the peoples they conquered.

The next time you come across a reference to mythology, remember the importance of these gods to the Romans and the immense cultural legacy they left us.

Fact 20 - 25 National Parks to Explore

Did you know that Italy is the nature sanctuary in Europe with its 25 breathtaking national parks? These natural treasures, spread from north to south, offer a diversity of breathtaking landscapes, from the Alpine summit to the Mediterranean coast.

Imagine strolling through the Cinque Terre National Park, where colorful villages meet turquoise seas. Or feel the fresh air of the Gran Paradiso National Park, Italy's oldest park, nestled in the Alps. These parks are gems, home to unique flora and fauna, and retaining the very essence of Italy's natural beauty.

But that's not all. Beyond their visual wonders, these parks play a vital role in protecting the environment. They are home to many endangered species and represent a delicate balance between nature conservation and public access.

So, on your next visit to Italy, don't settle for historic cities. Treat yourself to a getaway in the middle of nature and discover the green soul of Italy through its must-see national parks.

Fact 21 - Neapolitan pizza, a culinary legend

Have you ever heard of the real Neapolitan pizza, that culinary masterpiece born in Naples? This iconic dish, with its thin dough, fresh ingredients and unmistakable flavor, is much more than just a pizza. It is a piece of Italian history, shaped by centuries of tradition.

Its origin dates back to the days when the fishermen of Naples consumed bread pancakes topped with fresh tomatoes and cheese, creating a simple yet delicious recipe. One of the most famous anecdotes tells that the Margherita pizza was created in honor of Queen Margherita in 1889, with ingredients representing the colors of the Italian flag: red tomatoes, white mozzarella and green basil.

Neapolitan pizza is so precious that it was even listed as a UNESCO Intangible Heritage Site in 2017, highlighting its cultural significance. This recognition protects and honors the art of the Neapolitan pizzaiolos, who prepare this dish according to traditional methods.

So, on your next trip to Italy, don't forget to enjoy an authentic Neapolitan pizza. It's an experience that will awaken your taste buds and immerse you in the rich history of Italian cuisine.

Fact 22 - Caesar, Emperor Like No Other

Julius Caesar is an iconic figure in Roman history. But did you know that, contrary to popular belief, he was never emperor? It was actually Augustus, his adoptive, who would become the first emperor of Rome. Caesar, on the other hand, was a brilliant general, a talented orator, and a powerful dictator.

His military career is astonishing. His campaigns in Gaul, summarized in his work "Commentaries on the Gallic Wars", not only greatly enlarged the Roman territory, but also demonstrated his strategic genius. He was also remembered for crossing the Rubicon, a river, marking the beginning of a civil war that he would win.

In addition to his military exploits, Caesar introduced crucial political and social reforms, including the creation of the Julian calendar, still in use today in its Reformed form. This calendar corrected many of the mistakes of the previous Roman calendar, aligning more closely with the solar cycle.

The assassination of Caesar in 44 B.C. on the Ides of March by members of the Roman Senate marked the end of the Roman Republic and the beginning of imperial rule. His death and legacy have shaped the history of Rome and the Mediterranean world for centuries.

Fact 23 - The Enchanted Canals of Venice

Have you ever dreamed of sailing on the glittering canals of Venice, this city on the water? This unique set of canals and waterways forms the beating heart of the city. It was thanks to them that Venice was able to become a major maritime power during the Middle Ages and the Renaissance.

The Grand Canal, the most famous of these, winds its way through the city and offers stunning views of the historic palaces and stately buildings that line its banks. Vaporettos, a kind of floating bus, are constantly on the road, providing an essential mode of transport for locals and visitors alike.

But Venice's more discreet canals are just as charming. As you get lost in the maze of the city, you'll discover peaceful nooks and crannies, picturesque bridges and colorful facades that reflect their splendor in the water. It is in these less frequented places that you will truly feel the Venetian soul.

Gondolas, although touristy, remain a timeless symbol of Venice. Gliding across the water by a singing gondolier is a memorable experience, a dive into the timeless charm of this legendary city.

Fact 24 - The Renaissance, a New Golden Age

Do you know the importance of the Renaissance, the cultural movement that shook Europe between the 14th and 17th centuries? Its epicenter was in Italy, where artists, thinkers and scientists rediscovered the treasures of antiquity, laying the foundations for an era of renewal.

Florence, the birthplace of the Renaissance, saw the emergence of geniuses such as Leonardo da Vinci, Michelangelo and Botticelli. Their works, such as the Last Supper or the Sistine Chapel, are now considered true masterpieces. These artists were not simply painters, but polymaths, mastering a multitude of disciplines, from sculpture to engineering.

The Renaissance was not only a period of artistic progress. Minds like Galileo and Machiavelli laid the foundations for modern science and political thought. With the invention of the printing press, ideas spread like never before, ushering in a new era of knowledge.

So, the next time you admire a work of art from this period or reflect on the foundations of science and modern thought, remember that many of these advances took root in Italy, during the golden age of the Renaissance.

Fact 25 - The Hidden Treasures of Pompeii

Have you ever heard of the ancient city of Pompeii? This prosperous and bustling Roman city was abruptly buried in 79 AD. by the eruption of Mount Vesuvius. For centuries, Pompeii remained hidden, preserving beneath its ashes a frozen image of Roman life.

The excavations, which began in the 18th century, revealed entire streets, houses, temples and theatres. The casts of the victims' bodies, made from the cavities left by their decomposed bodies, offer a poignant testimony to their final moments. Vibrant frescoes of color still adorn the walls, and mosaics on the floor testify to the artistic richness of the era.

But Pompeii is not just an archaeological site. It is a direct testimony of the daily life of the Romans: shops, baths, inns... Every corner tells a story. You can even see the first wall advertisements and graffiti by citizens.

So, if you have the opportunity to visit this city frozen in time, immerse yourself in this window open to the past. You will discover, beyond the tragedies, the treasures and the daily life of a fascinating civilization.

Fact 26 - Romulus, Remus and a Founding Wolf

Do you know the fascinating history of the founding of Rome? It begins with two brothers, Romulus and Remus, abandoned in the Tiber by their uncle who wanted to seize the throne. Rescued from the waters by a flood, they were then suckled by a she-wolf in a cave, the Lupercal.

Raised by a shepherd, the two brothers grew up unaware of their royal ancestry. When they grew up, they decided to found a city. However, a disagreement over the ideal location divided them. Romulus wanted to build on the Palatine Hill while Remus preferred the Aventine Hill.

This dispute escalated into a conflict, and during an altercation, Romulus killed Remus. Becoming the sole master of the place, Romulus founded the city of Rome on the Palatine Hill in 753 BC, giving it his own name.

This legend, which mixes myth and history, is engraved in the Roman identity. As you visit the Eternal City, you'll be able to feel the power of this story that still resonates in the cobbled streets of Rome.

Fact 27 - Roman Tricks for Building Roads

Have you ever heard the saying "All roads lead to Rome"? It has its roots in the remarkable road network built by the Romans. In reality, these roads were much more than just a means of travel; they symbolized the immensity and power of the Roman Empire.

One of the major tricks of the Romans was to use a strict methodology. Each road was designed to be straight, regardless of distance, allowing for quick communication and travel. When they encountered a natural obstacle, such as a mountain, they built either around it or directly through it by digging tunnels.

The secret to the durability of these roads lies in their layered construction. The Romans first used coarse stones, then gravel, and finally paving stones for the surface. This method ensured good water drainage and increased the longevity of the road.

Even today, some of these roads exist and are in use, proof of their engineering excellence. As you walk around Italy, you may be walking in these historical tracks, witnesses of Roman genius.

Fact 28 - A Venetian Named Casanova

When you hear the name "Casanova", what do you think of? Surely to a charismatic seducer, isn't it? This is indeed the posthumous reputation of Giacomo Casanova, the eighteenth-century Venetian, but he was much more than that.

Casanova was born in Venice in 1725. Beyond his amorous conquests, he was an insatiable writer, spy, and traveler. He travelled all over Europe, going from court to court, rubbing shoulders with the nobility and intellectuals of his time.

His "Memoirs", written at the end of his life, are a fascinating testimony to European society in the eighteenth century. Through them, you can discover not only his love affairs, but also his thoughts on philosophy, culture, and even science.

So, the next time you hear the name "Casanova," remember that he wasn't just a playboy. He was a man of letters and wit, a privileged witness of his time, who left behind him a rich literary legacy.

Fact 29 - Sorbets and ice creams, thank you Italy!

Summer often rhymes with a delicious ice cream to cool off. But did you know that you owe a lot of this sweet treat to Italy? The country is at the origin of many innovations in ice creams and sorbets.

The earliest recipes for sorbets date back to ancient Sicily, where mountain snow mixed with fruit and sugar were used to create these refreshing delicacies. These sorbets were served at great feasts and were enjoyed by nobles and wealthy merchants.

It was in the sixteenth century that Florence played a crucial role in the evolution of ice. The famous architect Bernardo Buontalenti, in the service of the Medici, presented an ice cream at a banquet, which amazed the guests and laid the foundations for modern ice cream.

Today, whether it's a rich, creamy gelato in Rome or a tangy sorbet in Palermo, Italy continues to enchant taste buds around the world. So, during your next scoop of ice cream, don't forget to raise your cone in tribute to Italy!

Fact 30 - Italy's Enigmatic Bermuda Triangle

Have you ever heard of the Bermuda Triangle, that mysterious area where many ships and planes disappeared without a trace? Italy has its own similar mystery, often dubbed the "Italian Bermuda Triangle."

Located between Bologna, Florence and Rimini, this triangle has been the scene of many strange and unexplained phenomena. There are reports of bright lights in the sky, sudden power outages, and even unexplained disappearances of vehicles.

One of the most famous examples is that of a helicopter pilot in 1978, who reported being followed by an unidentified flying object before losing contact with the control tower. His helicopter was never found.

While scientists have put forward several theories, from terrestrial magnetism to subterranean gases, the mystery remains. So, if you travel to this region, keep your eyes open and maybe you'll be the next to witness a strange phenomenon in the Italian Bermuda Triangle!

Fact 31 - Sardinia, a paradise for wild horses

Do you know Sardinia? This Italian island is famous for its breathtaking beaches and delicious cuisine, but it also has a lesser-known treasure: wild horses. Indeed, this Mediterranean paradise is one of the few places in Europe where you can still observe these majestic creatures in the wild.

The "Cavallini della Giara" are an endemic breed of small horses that live on the Giara plateau. Despite their small size, they are robust and adapted to the harsh, rocky environment of the region. These horses have thick manes and dark coats that protect them from the scorching sun.

One of the most iconic times to see them is at dusk, when they descend to the waterholes to drink. Their graceful silhouette standing out against the Sardin landscape is a sight not to be missed.

So, if you're an adventurer and want to discover an unexpected side of Italy, don't hesitate to go to Sardinia. Who knows? You might be lucky and cross paths with these incredible wild horses.

Fact 32 - The Incredible Catacombs of Naples

Have you ever heard of the catacombs of Naples? Far from the hustle and bustle of the city, these ancient underground burials tell a rich and fascinating history. Dating back to the first Christian centuries, they stretch out in a mysterious labyrinth beneath vibrant Naples.

Carved out of tuff, a volcanic rock, these catacombs were originally burial sites for the city's first Christians. Each gallery, each niche, tells a story of love, faith and hope. Some frescoes and wall inscriptions, still visible today, will offer you a moving glimpse into these past lives.

One of the most famous is that of San Gennaro, the patron saint of Naples. According to legend, it was here that he was buried after his martyrdom, making this place an important pilgrimage center.

If you're visiting Naples, immerse yourself in these mystical depths. As you walk through the silent corridors of the catacombs, you'll connect with the ancient soul of this city, rich in history and secrets.

Fact 33 - Pinocchio, a Little Wooden Boy

Do you know the story of the boy whose nose grew longer every time he lied? It is the work of an Italian writer, Carlo Collodi, who in 1881 introduced the world to Pinocchio, the little boy made of wood by the carpenter Geppetto.

The story of Pinocchio is rich in life lessons. Through his misadventures, the young puppet seeks to become a real little boy. His mistakes, his encounters with various characters such as the Cat and the Fox, or the Blue-haired Fairy, remind us of the importance of truth and kindness.

Pinocchio's popularity has spread beyond Italy's borders. Thanks to a film adaptation by Disney in 1940, the tale has become a world reference. Who hasn't been touched by the sincerity of this character eager to win the love of his creator, Geppetto?

The next time you read or watch this story, remember that behind this fantastic tale lies the Italian literary genius, and a great lesson in personal growth and honesty.

Fact 34 - The Traditional Tarantella Dance

Have you ever heard of the tarantella? This vibrant and energetic dance has its origins in southern Italy, particularly Calabria, Campania and Sicily. Her catchy rhythms and fast movements captivate everyone who watches.

The story goes that this dance was born out of an old belief. It was thought that by dancing frantically, one could cure the bite of the tarantula, a local spider. Even though this idea may seem strange today, the dance has remained, transformed into a joyful and festive expression of Italian culture.

Nowadays, the tarantella is often played at feasts and celebrations, accompanied by instruments such as the tambourine and accordion. If you're attending a wedding in southern Italy, you'll surely get to see her in action, with guests forming circles, holding hands, and spinning in rhythm.

The next time you hear the catchy melody of the tarantella, let yourself be carried away by its energy. Maybe you'll even be tempted to join the dance and get carried away by this age-old tradition.

Fact 35 - Roman Aqueducts, the Art of Water

Did you know that the Roman Empire was the master of hydraulic engineering? The Romans built huge aqueducts that carried water over long distances to supply their cities with drinking water. These structures, often associated with impressive arches, are among the greatest achievements of antiquity.

One of the most notable examples is the Segovia Aqueduct in Spain. Even though it is not in Italy, it is a testament to the greatness of Roman architecture. In Italy, the Aqua Claudia, which stretched for more than 68 kilometers, carried water to the city of Rome, ensuring the supply for the baths and fountains.

Beyond their utilitarian function, these aqueducts were also architectural masterpieces. Precision-designed, they used gravity to circulate water, avoiding the need for pumps or other mechanisms.

If you travel to Italy, or other ancient Roman territories, you might still see the remains of these aqueducts. They will remind you of the ingenuity and vision of the Romans, who shaped history with their incredible engineering skills.

Fact 36 - The magic of Italian Christmas celebrations

Do you know the magic of Italian Christmas? In Italy, Christmas isn't just one day, it's a whole season brimming with traditions, culinary delights and fascinating stories. From the beginning of December, the streets light up and the Christmas markets open their doors, spreading a warm and festive atmosphere.

One of the most emblematic traditions is the "La Befana", a kind witch who brings gifts to children on January 6th, thus closing the festivities. According to legend, she is still looking for the baby Jesus after refusing to follow him with the Three Kings, later regretting her decision.

On a culinary level, the Christmas meal in Italy is a real feast. The "cenone", a big Christmas Eve dinner, is full of delicious dishes, such as the "tortellini in brodo" or the "panettone", a sweet candied fruit cake from Milan.

So, if you have the opportunity to experience Christmas in Italy, prepare to be amazed. Each region has its own traditions, guaranteeing a unique and unforgettable experience.

Fact 37 - The Invention of the Violin, an Italian Gift

Did you know that the violin, such an emblematic instrument, is a precious gift from Italy to the world? Its origins date back to the early sixteenth century, and it was in the regions of Lombardy and Piedmont that it came to life. These territories have become the cradle of this instrument that transformed classical music.

Italian craftsmen, with their know-how and passion, have refined and perfected the original design of the violin. One of the most famous luthiers, Antonio Stradivari, produced violins in Cremona that are now considered the best in the world. Some of his violins, nicknamed "Stradivarius", sell for several million euros at auction.

In Italy, classical music and the violin are inseparable. Prestigious schools such as the Accademia Nazionale di Santa Cecilia in Rome have trained eminent violinists who have shone on international stages.

So, the next time you listen to a violin melody, remember the rich Italian heritage behind every note and Italy's lasting impact on world music.

Fact 38 - The Medieval Ball Game "Calcio"

Before modern football conquered the world, Italy already had its own ball game, the "Calcio". Appearing in the sixteenth century in Florence, this game resembled a combination of rugby, football, and wrestling. Imagine yourself in Piazza Santa Croce, with two teams of 27 players challenging each other in an intense game of Calcio.

Each team was tasked with scoring as many points as possible by sending a leather ball into the opponent's goal. But be warned, the "Calcio" was not for the faint of heart. Punches were common, and anything goes, from tackles to punches. Some say it was more of a battlefield than a playground.

Historic matches have been held in honor of royal weddings and other major events. In 1530, during the siege of Florence, a Calcio match was even played to demonstrate the resilience and determination of the Florentines in the face of the enemy.

Today, this tradition continues with the "Calcio Storico", an annual event in Florence that celebrates this ancient game and shows the city's attachment to its historical roots.

Fact 39 - Secrets of the Hanging Gardens of Babylon

The Hanging Gardens of Babylon, one of the Seven Wonders of the Ancient World, are shrouded in mystery and wonder. Although not directly related to Italy, the influence of this marvel on Roman architecture and art is undeniable. Imagine verdant terraces gradually rising, creating the illusion of a lush mountain in the middle of a city.

King Nebuchadnezzar II is said to have had these gardens built in the sixth century BC. to soothe his wife, who came from a mountainous region, who was suffering from the flatness of the Mesopotamian landscape. The exact methods of their construction remain a mystery, but some theories suggest the use of advanced irrigation systems, such as the Archimedean screw, to provide water to plants.

Historical descriptions of these gardens speak of lush plants, fruit trees, and waterfalls, all fed by the Euphrates River. However, no concrete archaeological evidence of their existence has been found to date, adding to their mystical legend.

Although located far from Italy, the gardens have long inspired Italian artists and architects, evoking visions of paradise and human ingenuity that transcend borders and eras.

Fact 40 - The Giants of the Sartiglia Parade

Have you ever wondered what a horse race would be like with a carnival atmosphere? The Sartiglia, a traditional Sardinian parade, is the answer. This spectacular equestrian festival, which dates back to the 16th century, combines equestrian skill and festivities, providing an unforgettable spectacle for all who attend.

Every year in Oristano, talented riders compete in a frantic race to skewer a suspended star with a sword. But that's not all: the parade is also famous for its "masked giants" dancing in the streets. These majestic figures, dressed in traditional costumes, bring a mythical dimension to the event, evoking the ancient legends of the region.

But the Sartiglia is not just a demonstration of equestrian skill. It is also a symbol of Sardinian culture, mixing faith, superstition and tradition. Before the race, a blessing ceremony is held to ensure a year of prosperity for the community.

If you happen to be in Sardinia during this time, don't miss this fascinating celebration. It is a unique immersion into the deep soul of Italy, far from the beaten track and the usual tourist attractions.

Fact 41 - The Mysteries of the Island of Capri

Have you ever heard of the island of Capri, that jewel of the Bay of Naples? This small island has much more to offer than just panoramic views. It is shrouded in mysteries and legends that have attracted travelers for centuries.

One of the most famous points of interest on the island is the Grotta Azzurra, or the "Blue Grotto". Inside, the water glows an ethereal blue, creating an almost otherworldly atmosphere. According to some rumors, the cave was once the refuge of sea nymphs, mystical creatures that inhabited the depths.

But that's not all. The island was also the retreat of the Roman Emperor Tiberius. He built several villas on the island, including Villa Jovis, from where he ruled Rome. Dark stories surround this villa, with rumors of decadent feasts and mysterious disappearances.

When you visit Capri, let yourself be carried away by its mysterious charm. Between its bewitching caves and ancient legends, this Italian island is a real invitation to discovery and wonder.

Fact 42 - The Secrets of the Venetian Gondoliers

Did you know that behind every swing of a gondola in Venice there are centuries of traditions and secret techniques? Gondoliers are much more than just rowers; they are the guardians of the soul of Venice.

Each gondolier must undergo rigorous training before they can maneuver these elegant boats. They learn not only the art of rowing, but also the history of Venice and the many canals that crisscross it. It is knowledge passed down from generation to generation, often within the same family.

But the gondolier's job doesn't stop at rowing. These men often sing traditional serenades, adding a touch of magic to every ride. And yes, their melodious voice isn't just to charm tourists. It's a tradition reminiscent of the days when music floated in the Venetian air every night.

So, next time you're in Venice, hop on a gondola. Let yourself be lulled by the calm waters, listen to the stories that the gondolier has to tell you, and immerse yourself in the mysteries of this lakeside city.

Fact 43 - Italians' love for coffee

Have you ever enjoyed a real Italian espresso? In Italy, coffee is much more than just a drink, it's a way of life. From preparation to tasting, each step is carried out with passion and precision.

In the morning, Italians often start their day with a "cappuccino", preferring espresso for later in the day. If you go to a "bar" in Italy, you'll be surprised at how quickly the locals consume their coffee, often standing at the counter, chatting with the barista or reading the newspaper.

Italy is also home to many caffeinated specialties that the world loves, such as macchiato, ristretto or corretto (espresso "corrected" with a drop of liqueur). Each region, or even each city, has its own variant and tradition around coffee.

So, on your next visit to Italy, take the time to stop by a local café. Breathe in the mesmerizing aroma, sip slowly, and savor this experience deeply rooted in Italian culture.

Fact 44 - The Mystical Cimbri Forest

Have you ever heard of the Cimbri Forest in Italy? Located in the Veneto region, this forest is shrouded in mysteries and legends dating back to the time of the Cimbri, a Germanic people who settled here more than a millennium ago.

Nature in this forest is almost magical. Ancient trees and lush plants make it feel like you've stepped into another world. Some say that if you walk silently, you could hear the distant echoes of Cimbrian songs echoing through the trees.

But what makes this forest truly unique is its preserved culture. Despite their small population, the descendants of the Cimbri managed to preserve their language and traditions. Annual festivals celebrate this rich history, mixing music, dance and ancient tales.

Next time you visit Italy, consider a getaway to the Cimbri Forest. Let yourself be transported by its mystical atmosphere and discover a little-known, but fascinating, facet of Italy's rich cultural tapestry.

Fact 45 - The Talking Mountains of the Dolomites

Have you ever gazed at the majestic Dolomites, the mountains that stand like sentinels in northern Italy? These snow-capped peaks are not only famous for their beauty, but also for the legends they are home to, giving the impression that they have a voice of their own.

The formation of the Dolomites is a geological spectacle, with layers of rock that tell stories of ancient oceans and tectonic movements. But for the locals, these mountains also whisper the tales of the ancestors. Legends tell of kings and queens of stone, and of the fantastic creatures that inhabit these heights.

One of the most famous stories is that of the "Pale di San Martino", a rock formation that, according to legend, was once a vast meadow where witches gathered on nightly Sabbaths. Every evening, as the sun sets, the light gives a pink hue to the rocks, as if to recall these ancient stories.

Next time you visit the Dolomites, take a moment to listen. Perhaps you will hear the echoes of the legends that have shaped these extraordinary mountains.

Fact 46 - The Epic of Dante and his Inferno

Do you know Dante Alighieri? This illustrious Florentine poet of the Middle Ages is famous for his masterpiece, the "Divine Comedy". This epic is an adventure through the three realms of the afterlife: Hell, Purgatory, and Paradise. Hell, in particular, has captured the imagination of many generations.

The "Divine Comedy" begins with Dante's journey through the nine circles of Hell, where he meets various sinners undergoing punishments appropriate to their sins. Guided by the ancient poet Virgil, Dante accurately and passionately describes each scene, such as that of the adulterous lovers, Paolo and Francesca, swirling eternally in an infernal storm.

But why did Dante write this work? Exiled from his beloved Florence, he composed this poem as a meditation on good, evil, and the human condition. His vision of Hell is a bold critique of the society of his time, evoking well-known political and ecclesiastical figures.

The next time you delve into Italian literature, remember Dante. His Inferno is more than just a story: it's a window into the Italian soul and culture.

Fact 47 - The Legendary Heroes of Abruzzo

In the heart of Italy, the wild mountains of Abruzzo are home to stories and legends that have spanned the centuries. These rich and fascinating tales tell of legendary heroes, fantastic beasts and epic adventures. Have you ever wondered where these tales come from?

One of the most famous legends is that of Theophilus, a pious man who, betrayed by unrequited love, makes a pact with the devil. But, with the help of the Virgin Mary, he manages to recover his soul. This story is often told at vigils, evoking themes of love, betrayal, and redemption.

Abruzzo also holds stories of mythical creatures. Like Scanno's werewolf, a cursed man who transforms at the full moon, or the mountain spirits that protect villages from intruders.

As you visit this area, you will feel the presence of these legends around every corner. They are an integral part of Abruzzo's cultural identity, a testament to the imaginative richness and passion of Italians for epic tales.

Fact 48 - The bright colours of Burano

If you head to the Venetian lagoon, a dazzling island is sure to catch your eye: Burano. Unlike its neighbours, this small island stands out for its multicoloured houses, lined up along picturesque canals. But do you know why Burano shines brightly?

Legend has it that local fishermen would paint their houses with bright colors to spot them from afar when they returned from fishing in the thick fog of the lagoon. These luminous hues, which have become iconic, guided their path, illuminating their homecoming.

But it's not just for its colors that Burano is famous. The island is also known for its exquisite lace, an art passed down from generation to generation. The women of Burano, while their husbands were at sea, delicately wove this lace, contributing to the island's international fame.

On your next visit to Italy, be sure to stop off in Burano. Stroll through its narrow streets, admire the symphony of colours and feel the authentic soul of a place where tradition and beauty intertwine at every step.

Fact 49 - The Art of Opera at La Scala in Milan

Have you ever heard of La Scala in Milan? It's one of the most iconic opera houses in the world, and if you're a lover of opera, it's a place not to be missed. Nestled in the heart of Milan, this theatre has hosted the biggest names in opera since its creation in 1778.

La Scala is not just a stage, it is a sanctuary of music. Legends such as Luciano Pavarotti, Maria Callas and Arturo Toscanini have all walked its boards, leaving an indelible mark. Here, every note resonates with a story, every performance is emotionally charged.

But what makes La Scala so unique isn't just the quality of the performances. It's also the building's grandiose architecture and exceptional acoustics, which have been carefully crafted to capture every musical nuance. The interior, with its red velvets and sparkling golds, transports the viewer to a world of refinement and passion.

If you're in Milan, make a promise: book an evening to attend an opera at La Scala. Let yourself be carried away by the magic, and feel the strength of history and tradition that permeates every corner of this mythical place.

Fact 50 - The Mysteries of Lake Como

Have you ever dreamed of mesmerizing landscapes, majestic mountains and reflections of water shimmering in the sun? Lake Como, located in Lombardy, is exactly that dream embodiment. Its deep waters, the deepest of all Italian lakes, hide many secrets and have inspired generations of artists, writers and travellers.

The inverted "Y" shaped lake is surrounded by opulent villas and lush gardens that date back to the Roman period. For example, the Villa del Balbianello, which has been used as a setting for films such as "Star Wars" and "James Bond", will reveal its sumptuous gardens and panoramic views. It's a glimpse of the glamour that has always been associated with this region.

But there's more to Como than its apparent beauty. Immerse yourself in its legends, such as that of the "Bella Pescatrice", the beautiful fisherwoman who, it is said, still haunts its waters, looking for a lost love. These stories add a mystical dimension to the serenity of the place.

Next time you're looking for a place to get away from it all, consider Lake Como. Let yourself be charmed by its mysteries, natural beauty, and rich history, and you'll understand why so many hearts have been captured by this Italian gem.

Fact 51 - Stone giants in the Alps

You've probably heard of the majestic Alps, the mountains that dominate part of Europe. But did you know that, hidden in these Italian mountains, there are silent giants made of stone? These rock formations, sculpted by time and the elements, bear an uncanny resemblance to human or animal figures, adding a touch of mystery to this already awe-inspiring landscape.

One of the most famous is "Il Gigante", located near the city of Courmayeur. This huge rock formation resembles a sleeping man, and locals tell stories about this "giant" who is said to have protected the valley for millennia. Tourists and climbers are often amazed by this imposing presence silhouetted against the sky.

Walking further afield, you might also come across the "Cavallo di Pietra" (Stone Horse) in the Gran Paradiso National Park. Some say it is the depiction of a horse turned to stone for defying the mountain gods.

These stone giants, silent witnesses to the history of the Alps, remind you how powerful and mysterious nature is. They add an almost mythological dimension to these mountains, making every hike in the Italian Alps even more memorable.

Fact 52 - The Mysterious Treasure of Ostia

Have you ever dreamed of hunting for a hidden treasure? Ostia, the ancient port of Rome, is full of mysteries and fascinating stories, one of which concerns a lost treasure. According to local legends, a huge treasure is buried somewhere in the ruins of this ancient city, patiently waiting to be discovered.

Over the centuries, many adventurers and archaeologists have tried their luck to find this treasure. Ancient accounts tell of a Roman ship that was laden with gold and other riches, and sank near the port of Ostia during a violent storm. Although numerous excavations have been undertaken, the treasure remains untraceable to this day.

The town itself is an archaeological gem, with its cobbled streets, thermal baths and theatres that are a testament to its prosperous past. But for many, it is the allure of this hidden treasure that gives Ostia such a special aura.

So, if you're in an adventurous mood and visiting Italy, why not head to Ostia? Who knows, maybe you'll be the lucky one to get your hands on this legendary treasure and finally solve this age-old mystery.

Fact 53 - The Incredible Legend of Rialto

Have you ever crossed the Rialto Bridge in Venice? In addition to being an architectural masterpiece, this bridge hides an incredible legend. According to a local story, this bridge was the result of a pact with the devil himself. Yes, you read that right!

In the 16th century, when Venice was looking to build a stone bridge to replace the original wooden bridge, the technical challenges were numerous. An architect named Antonio da Ponte was said to have been so desperate to complete the project that he appealed to the devil for help. In exchange, the devil asked for the first soul to cross the bridge.

The bridge was completed, defying all expectations. To deceive the devil, Antonio let a rooster loose on the deck, offering his innocent soul in place of a human being. Even today, some claim to hear the crowing of a rooster near the Rialto at dawn, reminiscent of the architect's clever subterfuge.

The next time you're standing on that iconic bridge, think about this fascinating story. Maybe you'll feel the magic and mystery that surrounds this historic place.

Fact 54 - Sicilian Puppets

Have you ever heard of the "teatro dei pupi"? It is not just a theatre, but a tradition that is deeply rooted in Sicily. For centuries, Sicilian puppets have been telling epic stories, romances and legendary battles, captivating audiences of all ages.

Each puppet is carefully carved, ornate, and clothed, reflecting a specific character, whether it's a heroic knight or a fearsome monster. These characters often come from the "Chansons de geste", a series of medieval poems celebrating the exploits of Christian knights. For example, Orlando and Rinaldo, two folk heroes, are frequently depicted in these shows.

But it's not just the art of puppetry that fascinates. It is also the way in which the puppeteers, with passion and skill, bring these characters to life. Every movement is precise, every scene is set to music and song, transforming the show into an immersive experience.

If you ever go to Sicily, don't miss the opportunity to attend a performance. Let yourself be carried away by the adventures of Sicilian puppets and discover a living piece of Italy's cultural history.

Fact 55 - The Wonderful History of Tiramisu

Do you know the dessert that has captivated taste buds around the world with its creamy sweetness and exquisite blend of coffee, mascarpone and cocoa? Yes, that's Tiramisu! But do you know where it really comes from?

Originating in the Veneto region of Italy, tiramisu, whose name means "pull me up" or "cheer me up," originated in the 1960s. Although there are many legends surrounding its creation, the most popular one relates that it was served to Venetian courtesans to give them energy.

The traditional recipe is simple yet exquisite: spoon biscuits dipped in espresso coffee, layered with delicious mascarpone cream and sprinkled with bitter cocoa. Each bite is an explosion of flavors that dances in harmony in the mouth.

Next time you enjoy this dessert, remember its rich Italian heritage. Behind each spoonful lies a story of love, tradition and pure indulgence. And don't forget to say "grazie" to Italy for this incomparable delicacy!

Fact 56 - The Guardian of the Alps, the Ibex

Have you ever heard of the majestic animal that reigns supreme on the rugged peaks of the Italian Alps? The ibex, also known as the Alpine ibex, is the silent guardian that overlooks valleys and precipices with grace and agility.

This robust animal, recognizable by its long, curved horns, originated in the Alpine mountains, where it evolved to face the harshest conditions. Its split hooves give it exceptional grip, allowing it to climb near-vertical walls with disconcerting ease.

Unfortunately, the ibex has been hunted almost to extinction for its horns and meat. Fortunately, thanks to conservation efforts in Italy and other parts of the Alps, its population has recovered and it is now a symbol of nature's triumph over adversity.

Next time you're in the Italian Alps, look up and look for that iconic guardian. Its presence is a reminder of the rugged beauty and resilience of nature, and the vital role Italy plays in protecting it.

Fact 57 - The Explorer Amerigo Vespucci

Do you know where the name "America" comes from? It has its roots in the name of a daring Italian explorer, Amerigo Vespucci. Born in Florence in 1454, Amerigo quickly established himself as a central figure in voyages of discovery to the New World.

Vespucci was not only a navigator, but also a skilled cartographer. Unlike many of his contemporaries, he quickly realized that the lands discovered by Christopher Columbus were not Asia, but a new continent hitherto unknown to Europeans. His meticulous work helped map these newly discovered regions with an accuracy unmatched for the time.

His travels to South America were so influential that, when German cartographer Martin Waldseemüller created a map of the New World in 1507, he suggested that the continent be named in honor of Amerigo. That's how "America" was born.

Thanks to Vespucci, Italy not only left its mark on the world map, but it also cemented its reputation as a nation of daring explorers and forward-thinking thinkers.

Fact 58 - The Delicious Secret of Risotto

Do you know the iconic dish that Italians cherish as much as their pasta? It's risotto, a creamy rice preparation that awakens the taste buds. Originating in northern Italy, specifically the Lombardy region, risotto has a history as rich as its taste.

The secret of risotto lies in the type of rice used: Arborio, Carnaroli or Vialone Nano. These varieties, grown in the fertile regions of the Po Valley, are known for their ability to absorb liquids while maintaining a slightly firm core. Thanks to this feature, they can be cooked with broth to achieve that characteristic creamy texture.

But it's not just the rice that makes the magic. The cooking method is essential. You need to add the broth slowly, stirring constantly, to release the starch from the rice. It is this meticulous attention that gives risotto its unique consistency.

The next time you're enjoying a bowl of risotto, think about the history and tradition behind every bite. It's a true celebration of Italian culinary art.

Fact 59 - The Magic of the Roman Circus

Have you ever heard of the Circus Maximus of Rome? Before you imagine clowns or acrobats, know that the "circus" in Roman times had a completely different meaning. It was a vast space dedicated to chariot racing, one of the most popular forms of entertainment in ancient Rome.

Located between the Palatine Hills and the Aventine Hills, the Circus Maximus could accommodate up to 250,000 spectators. Imagine the crowd cheering on their favorite teams, the charioteers deftly wielding their floats around the spinae, ornate obstacles located in the middle of the track.

But it wasn't just a sports venue. The circus was also a place where religious events and celebrations were held. For example, during the festival of Consualia, chariot races were held in honor of the god Consus, protector of granaries.

So, the next time you think of the "circus", remember the importance it had in Roman culture, long before the emergence of the circus as we know it today.

Fact 60 - The Riddle of the Mantuan Labyrinth

Would it have occurred to you that a labyrinth could hide centuries-old secrets? The labyrinth of Mantua, nestled in the gardens of Palazzo Ducale, has been shrouded in mystery and legend since its creation. Designed in the 16th century, this maze is much more than just a game to lose visitors.

Its complex form has often been interpreted as a representation of the quest for truth and knowledge. The center of the labyrinth is believed to symbolize the attainment of wisdom. It is said that those who reach the heart of the labyrinth find a revelation there.

In addition, rumors have circulated that the labyrinth was used as a secret meeting place for lovers or even as a hiding place for treasures. Although these stories have never been confirmed, they add a layer of mystery to the place.

So, if you find yourself in Mantua, will you dare to venture into this labyrinth? Who knows what you might discover or feel as you walk its winding paths.

Fact 61 - The Dance of the Stars in San Lorenzo

Have you ever been amazed by the beauty of the night sky? In Italy, every year around August 10, the sky lights up with a thousand lights for the "Night of San Lorenzo", also known as the "Night of the Shooting Stars". The shooting stars you see that night are associated with the Perseid meteor shower.

Legend has it that these stars are actually tears of San Lorenzo. Martyred and died on 10 August, he shed, according to popular belief, tears in the form of shooting stars. By making a wish when a shooting star crosses the sky, it is said that San Lorenzo will grant your wish.

Across Italy, families and friends gather to observe this celestial phenomenon, often lying on blankets with picnic baskets. It's a moment of magic, hope and daydreaming.

The next time you're in Italy at this time, don't forget to roll your eyes. Maybe San Lorenzo will grant you a wish during this star dance.

Fact 62 - The Mystery of Alberobello's Trulli

Have you ever heard of trulli, those little white houses with conical roofs that look like they came straight out of a fairy tale? These amazing constructions are mainly found in Alberobello, in the Puglia region of southern Italy.

The special thing about trulli is their design. Built without any mortar, these shelters are made only of stacked dry stones. This centuries-old technique allowed the people of Alberobello to quickly dismantle their homes to escape taxes imposed by the Spanish monarchy, which ruled the area at the time.

Behind their simple appearance lies a rich history. The roofs of trulli are often adorned with pagan or Christian symbols, which are believed to bring good luck or protect the house. These symbols, carved directly into the stone, reflect the beliefs and traditions of the people of Puglia.

Next time you're visiting Italy, don't miss the opportunity to visit Alberobello. Walking between these ancestral homes will make you feel like you've been transported to another world, both mystical and wonderful.

Fact 63 - The melodies of Verdi and Puccini

Have you ever been swept away by a haunting melody, where every note seems to tell a story? If so, there's a good chance you've crossed paths with the works of two giants of Italian classical music: Verdi and Puccini.

Giuseppe Verdi, born in the early 19th century, is the composer behind memorable operas like "La Traviata" or "Rigoletto". His works, imbued with emotion and drama, revolutionized opera. Take "Nabucco" for example, whose chorus "Va, pensiero" became a hymn to freedom for Italians, especially during their quest for unification.

A few decades later, Giacomo Puccini took over with masterpieces like "La Bohème", "Tosca" or "Madama Butterfly". His ability to weave captivating melodies and touching stories has made him one of the most performed composers in the world.

The next time you listen to an opera or attend a performance, let yourself be carried away by the notes of these Italian masters. Their timeless music continues to move and inspire generations of listeners.

Fact 64 - The Subterranean Wonders of Sardinia

Do you know the secrets hidden in the soil of Sardinia? Underneath this Mediterranean island, an underground world stretches out, consisting of amazing caves and caverns, offering a breathtaking natural spectacle.

Among the most famous is the "Grotta del Bue Marino", accessible by sea. Its limestone walls, sculpted by water over millennia, give rise to strange and fascinating formations. In the past, this place was the refuge of monk seals, hence its name.

Not far from there, "Su Meraculu", a lesser-known cave, surprises with its stalactites and stalagmites with surreal shapes. Walking through its halls, you feel like you're entering a natural cathedral, where every nook and cranny tells a story thousands of years old.

So, next time you visit Sardinia, don't settle for its paradisiacal beaches. Dare to dive into its depths to discover a mysterious and bewitching universe, where nature has fashioned wonders out of sight.

Fact 65 - The Fable of King Midas in Sicily

Did you know that the legend of King Midas, although originating in Greek antiquity, has left an indelible mark on Sicily? Mythology is full of tales that transcend borders, and Midas' is no different.

Legend has it that Midas, after saving a friend of the god Dionysus, is granted a wish. Blinded by greed, he wants everything he touches to turn to gold. But his gift soon turns out to be a curse. Imagine, even the food he tries to eat becomes solid gold!

In Sicily, local tales tell of places where Midas is said to have stayed, leaving behind traces of his unfortunate ability. Some say that some golden stones found in the area are the tears of Midas, petrified by his own desire.

So, as you travel through Sicily and stumble upon a golden glow under the Mediterranean sun, remember the story of Midas, a reminder that sometimes, the deepest desires can turn against us.

Fact 66 - The Secrets of Bolognese Sauce

Have you ever wondered where exactly the famous Bolognese sauce that so many of us love comes from? Its origin can be traced back to the city of Bologna, in the Emilia-Romagna region of Italy. The traditional recipe is much richer and more varied than you might imagine.

Unlike many international versions that favor tomato, the real Bolognese sauce, called "Ragù alla Bolognese," is actually made with finely ground beef, onions, celery, carrots, and a little tomato. It simmers for hours to reach a rich and flavorful consistency.

Another interesting fact: although many associate this sauce with spaghetti, in Italy it is traditionally served with tagliatelle, a wider pasta that holds this thick sauce better. It is also a key ingredient in lasagna.

Next time you feast on a pasta Bolognese dish, remember its rich Italian heritage and consider trying the authentic recipe to get a taste of Bologna's culinary history.

Fact 67 - The Treasures of Hadrian's Villa

You've probably heard of the Roman emperors, but do you know Hadrian's villa? Located in Tivoli, near Rome, this imperial residence was built in the 2nd century AD. for Emperor Hadrian. It was much more than just a villa; It was a real small town in itself, with its thermal baths, theatres, palaces and gardens.

Imagine strolling through a complex stretching over 120 hectares. Hadrian, a traveling emperor, designed his villa to reflect the different cultures he had discovered during his travels. For example, there is the "Canopus", inspired by an Egyptian sanctuary, and the "Greek Baths" with their Hellenistic design.

One of the most captivating wonders of this villa is the "Maritime Theatre", a circular structure surrounded by water where Hadrian retired to seek tranquility. It is a miniature private island, a reflection of his love for the sea and architecture.

Next time you visit Rome, don't forget to take a detour to this archaeological wonder. It will give you a unique insight into Hadrian's greatness and vision.

Fact 68 - Legends of the Blue Caves

Have you ever dreamed of a place where the water glows an ethereal, almost unreal sapphire blue color? This is exactly what you will discover when you visit the Grotta Azzurra (Blue Grotto) on the island of Capri. It is a natural spectacle, where the sun's rays, penetrating through an underwater opening, illuminate the interior of the cave with a blue glow.

The beauty of this cave has given rise to countless legends. One of them claims that the cave was the temple of sea nymphs, deities who are said to have inhabited these mystical waters. It is said that those who entered were captivated by their song and could never leave.

Another legend tells of a secret passage leading to the palace of the Queen of the Seas. For centuries, local fishermen feared this cave, considering it cursed and avoiding entering it. It is for this reason that the cave remained largely unexplored until the 19th century.

Today, you can explore this natural wonder by boat, and let yourself be enveloped by the magic and mysteries of the Grotta Azzurra. Who knows, maybe you'll be lucky enough to hear the nymphs' song?

Fact 69 - The Charm of Roman Villas

Do you know those magnificent mansions that dot the Italian countryside, eloquent testimonies of the grandeur of ancient Rome? These are the Roman villas, luxurious residences designed for the elites of the time. Each villa is a true architectural masterpiece, reflecting the refined taste and social status of its owner.

Imagine, for example, the Villa dei Quintili in Rome. Located on the famous Via Appia, it once covered more than 4 km², with its thermal baths, fountains and extensive gardens. It wasn't just a house; It was a symbol of power and prestige. These villas were often the center of vast agricultural estates, and they played a vital role in the Roman economy.

But that's not all. Inside these villas, you'll discover dazzling mosaics, murals, and sculptures that give us a glimpse into the daily lives, beliefs, and passions of their inhabitants.

Today, these villas are open-air museums, places where you can walk in the footsteps of the past, breathe in history and lose yourself in the splendor of ancient Rome.

Fact 70 - The Wolves of Lazio

Have you ever heard of the legends surrounding wolves in the Lazio region? This region, where the Eternal City of Rome is located, has always been closely linked to these mysterious creatures. It is in this region that the story of Romulus and Remus, the legendary founders of Rome, took root, a story inseparable from the presence of a she-wolf.

Legend has it that this she-wolf rescued and fed the abandoned twins, Romulus and Remus, at the foot of the Palatine. This story has become so iconic that you can see the image of the she-wolf suckling the twins on many Roman monuments and coins. It symbolizes strength, perseverance, and protection.

But it's not just a legend. Lazio is still home to wolves in the wild. Despite urban pressure and landscape changes, these majestic animals have managed to survive and adapt to their environment.

Next time you're walking in the hills of Lazio, keep your eyes peeled. Maybe you'll be lucky enough to spot one of these wolves, silent witnesses to the region's thousand-year-old history.

Fact 71 - The Mystery of the Sphinxes of Rome

Have you ever wondered why, while walking around Rome, you sometimes come across the majestic silhouette of a sphinx? These mythical creatures, usually associated with ancient Egypt, found a surprising place in Roman architecture and art.

Rome's interest in Egypt increased after the conquest of that territory in 30 BC. Subsequently, many Egyptian obelisks and other artifacts were transported to Rome, and the Sphinx, a symbol of mystery and power, began to appear in the Italian capital. You can, for example, observe these enigmatic creatures carved on sarcophagi, frescoes, and even Roman villas.

Sphinxes are not simply decorative elements; They represent the fusion of Roman and Egyptian cultures. The inclusion of this symbol shows how open Rome was to assimilating and celebrating the cultures of its conquered territories.

Next time you visit Rome, be amazed by these silent guardians who, perched on their pedestals, tell a story of conquest, admiration, and cultural fusion.

Fact 72 - The Exploits of Hannibal and His Elephants

Have you heard of the incredible journey of Hannibal, the Carthaginian general who led his troops across the Alps to attack ancient Rome? His audacity doesn't stop there: he achieved this feat in the company of war elephants.

In 218 B.C., Hannibal decided to invade Italy via the north, an unexpected route. Rather than choosing the seaway or the plains, he opted for a mountainous route, despite the many challenges it presented. This tactical choice was intended to surprise the Romans, and it succeeded.

But the elephants weren't just there for the show. In ancient battles, these giants were terrifying war machines, capable of sowing panic in the enemy ranks. Hannibal, aware of their impact, skillfully used them during his campaigns in Italy.

However, the Alps got the better of many of these majestic creatures. Even so, the image of Hannibal crossing the mountains with his elephants has become legendary, symbolizing his determination and innovative military strategy in the face of Roman power.

Fact 73 - The Ballet of Summer Shooting Stars

Every summer, the Italian sky offers a breathtaking spectacle. Have you ever had the chance to watch the dance of shooting stars from a Tuscan hill or a seaside in Sardinia? If you don't, you're missing out on a memorable experience.

The peak of this celestial phenomenon occurs around August 12, during the Perseid meteor shower. These stars, which appear to emerge from the constellation Perseus, are actually debris from Comet Swift-Tuttle entering the Earth's atmosphere and bursting into flames under friction.

Italy, with its clear skies and many panoramic viewpoints, is the perfect place to watch this celestial ballet. Regions such as Tuscany or Sardinia offer exceptional opportunities to admire these bright flashes, away from the light pollution of big cities.

So, the next time you're in Italy in August, don't forget to look up at the sky and make a wish for every shooting star you see. It is a tradition that many respect and cherish.

Fact 74 - The Hidden Art of Roman Mosaics

Walking around Italy, you have certainly come across splendid mosaics that adorn many archaeological sites. These meticulously assembled pieces of art tell ancient stories, silent witnesses of the Roman era.

The mosaic technique was highly prized by the Romans. Each small piece of colored stone or glass, called a "tesserae," was carefully chosen and placed to form scenes, patterns, or portraits. For example, the Villa del Casale in Sicily is home to one of the largest and most impressive collections of Roman mosaics, depicting scenes ranging from everyday life to mythology.

But what makes this art so special is its power of preservation. Thanks to the strength of the materials used, many mosaics have survived almost intact for centuries. As a result, they provide us with valuable insight into the culture, beliefs and everyday life of the Roman Empire.

The next time you come across one of these mosaics, take a moment to admire the skill and patience of the artists who, stone by stone, have created these timeless masterpieces.

Fact 75 - The Poetry of the Fountains of Rome

Walking around Rome is like flipping through a book of poetry with every page carved in stone. The fountains of the Eternal City, through their beauty and history, add an undeniable magic to its streets and squares.

Take for example the famous Fontana di Trevi. Not only is it an architectural masterpiece, but it is also steeped in tradition. According to legend, throwing a coin into the fountain guarantees your return to the Italian capital. Thousands of travelers take part in this ritual every day, captivated by the aura of this fountain.

But there's more to Rome than just the Fontana di Trevi. Around every corner, you'll discover more discreet, but equally bewitching fountains. Each one has its own story, its own charm, from the Barcaccia located at the foot of the Spanish Steps to the Fontana delle Tartarughe which depicts angels and turtles.

So, as you walk through Rome, let yourself be seduced by the murmur of the water and the stories carved in stone. These fountains are much more than just watering holes; They are the beating heart of the city.

Fact 76 - The Tale of the Mermaids of Amalfi

Have you ever heard of the mysterious mermaids of Amalfi? These legendary creatures are deeply rooted in the tales and legends of this picturesque coast of Italy. According to mythology, they used their melodious songs to bewitch sailors, luring them to the depths of the sea.

One of the most famous stories tells of the hero Odysseus, curious to hear the song of the sirens, ordered his crew to plug their ears and tie them to the mast of his ship. Thus, he could listen to their haunting song without being tempted to dive into the sea. With each note, he was more captivated, proof of the irresistible power of these creatures.

Today, the Amalfi Coast is famous for its breathtaking landscapes, picturesque villages, and azure waters. But when you wander around, listen: perhaps you will hear the distant echo of the siren song.

The next time you sail near Amalfi, remember the legends that cradle these waters. Every wave could hide a secret, every echo could be a siren's song.

Fact 77 - The Fascinating History of Limoncello

Did you know that limoncello, that delicious lemony liqueur, originates from the beautiful Amalfi Coast in Italy? Its history is as sunny as its vibrant taste. Although its exact origins are shrouded in mystery, there are several fascinating stories circulating about it.

Legend has it that, as early as the early twentieth century, the inhabitants of the island of Capri offered limoncello to distinguished guests. They used the secret recipe of their ancestors, macerating the lemon peels in alcohol and then adding sugar to sweeten the mixture. Thus, an intoxicating and refreshing beverage was born.

The other popular narrative suggests that fishermen and farmers in the area made this drink to protect themselves from the morning cold. They quickly discovered that limoncello was not only beneficial against the cold, but also a great digestif after a hearty Italian meal.

Today, limoncello is loved all over the world, but nowhere is it as delicious as on the terrace of an Italian café, with the view of the sparkling sea. Next time you try it, remember its sunny history.

Fact 78 - The Miracles of St. Francis of Assisi

Have you ever heard of St. Francis of Assisi? He is one of the most revered religious figures in Italy, recognized for his many miracles and his life dedicated to simplicity and compassion. Born in 1181, Francis renounced a life of wealth to follow a path of humility and devotion.

One of his most famous miracles is the "preaching to the birds." It is said that, during one of his meditations, Francis approached a group of birds. Instead of flying away, the birds came closer and listened to him as he told them the praises of God, symbolizing the harmony between man and nature.

Another memorable tale is that of "stigma." Towards the end of his life, Francis is said to have received the stigmata of Christ, bearing the marks of the wounds on his hands, feet, and side, reflecting his deep spiritual connection and devotion.

Today, Assisi, his hometown, is a place of pilgrimage for many believers from all over the world. As you walk through the medieval alleys, you can feel the peaceful presence of this saint who has so influenced the history of Italy.

Fact 79 - The Legends of the Italian Lakes

Italy's lakes are much more than just glistening bodies of water. Each lake is steeped in stories and legends that make them mystical places. Have you ever heard of the Lake Garda monster? According to local legends, a mysterious aquatic creature, similar to the Loch Ness Monster, inhabits the depths of the lake.

Lake Como, on the other hand, contains the legend of the "Bella Gigogin", a beautiful woman who is said to have appeared on the shores of the lake on full moon nights. Its haunting melody would draw men into the waters, where they would disappear forever. Many claim to have heard its melodious songs on silent nights.

Further south, Lake Bolsena is associated with a sacred history. It is said that in the 13th century, a priest witnessed a Eucharistic miracle there, where a host bled on a cloth, leaving an imprint that is now preserved in Orvieto.

The next time you're standing by one of these lakes, take a moment to listen to the whispers of the past. Perhaps you will hear an echo of the legends that still haunt these tranquil waters.

Fact 80 - The Delicate Art of Venetian Mosaic

When you walk around Venice, one of the things that immediately catches your eye is the dazzling Venetian mosaic. These masterpieces, made of tiny pieces of coloured glass or "tesserae", are the reflection of a know-how that has endured through the centuries.

Perhaps the greatest example of this art is St. Mark's Basilica. Upon entering, you will find yourself enveloped by more than 8000 square meters of brilliant mosaics, telling biblical stories and legends. These luminescent images almost seem to float, providing an almost celestial experience for visitors.

It is no coincidence that Venice has become the cradle of this art. Thanks to its strategic position, the city had access to rare and valuable materials, and its craftsmen quickly mastered the art of transforming these materials into beautiful pictorial representations.

Next time you're in Venice, take some time to admire these mosaics. Each tessera, each color, tells a story of devotion, trade, and craftsmanship that has shaped the Serenissima for millennia.

Fact 81 - The wonderful island of Elba

The island of Elba, nestled in the heart of the Tyrrhenian Sea, is the third largest islet in Italy. When you discover it, you will immediately be seduced by its golden beaches, green hills and crystal clear waters that offer shades ranging from deep blue to bright turquoise.

Historically speaking, the island is probably best known as the place of exile of Napoleon Bonaparte in 1814. During the ten months he spent there, Napoleon was not content to remain inactive: he transformed the island, improving the infrastructure and bringing with him a wind of reform. His residence, Villa dei Mulini, is now a museum that you can visit to immerse yourself in this fascinating period.

In addition to its history, the island of Elba offers unspoilt nature, with hiking trails that wind through its mountains and forests, offering stunning panoramic views. Its waters are also teeming with life, making it a paradise for diving enthusiasts.

So, if you're looking for a mix of history, natural beauty, and adventure, Elba is a must-see destination during your stay in Italy.

Fact 82 - The Amazing History of Brioche

Ah, the brioche! That delicious soft and airy bread that you might enjoy for breakfast with a little jam or butter. But did you know that its history is intrinsically linked to Italy? Let's dive into his gourmet tale together.

Brioche actually has its roots in "Pan Briaca", a sweet and spicy Italian medieval bread. Over the centuries, the recipe has morphed, incorporating ingredients like butter, giving rise to that soft and delicate texture you know well. It was in Milan that this evolution largely took shape, especially with the "Panettone", a local variant.

In the seventeenth century, brioche made its way to France, especially thanks to Italian queens who married French kings. It quickly became a staple on royal tables and, subsequently, on French bakeries.

So, every time you enjoy a slice of brioche, you taste a piece of history that unites Italy and France. A beautiful fusion of cultures and flavors to enjoy!

Fact 83 - The fairy tale of the Aosta Valley

The Aosta Valley, with its majestic mountains and deep forests, is the scene of many legends. Among them, that of the fairies of this valley will transport you to a magical world. Ready to travel to the heart of Italian myths?

It is said that in the past, fairies lived in the dense forests of the valley, guardians of the secrets of the mountains. These mystical beings, clad in sparkling robes, danced on full moon nights, leaving behind a trail of silver sparkles. For example, near the town of Cogne, witnesses claim to have seen strange lights, perhaps the remains of these fairytale dances.

But these fairies were not just figures of the night. They were said to help the inhabitants of the valley in times of need, for example by guiding wayward travellers or offering valuable advice to those who ventured into the mountains.

Next time you visit the Aosta Valley, keep your eyes open and your ears open. Who knows? Perhaps the whisper of the wind or the twinkling of a star will reveal to you some of this ancient and wonderful history.

Fact 84 - The Legend of the Carrara Caves

The mountains of Carrara in Tuscany are famous for their pure white marble. But did you know that, hidden in these mountains, there are ancient caves surrounded by legends? Let's dive into one of them together.

The most popular of these stories is about a fairy named "Bianca", who is said to have lived in these caves. According to the accounts, its beauty was as dazzling as the marble itself. Sculptors, captivated by its beauty, came from far and wide to try to capture it in stone. Michelangelo himself is said to have been inspired by this legend when he chose Carrara marble to sculpt the David.

But Bianca wasn't just a muse for artists. Legend has it that she also protected miners. When the tunnels became dangerous, his melodious voice resonated, guiding workers to safety, safe from impending landslides.

So, on your next visit to Carrara, as you travel through these white mountains, listen carefully. Maybe Bianca's song will still resonate, mixed with the sound of the wind and the echoes of the mountain.

Fact 85 - The magic of the feast of San Gennaro

Ah, Naples! Known for its pizza, Vesuvius and... the miracle of San Gennaro. Did you know that every year, this coastal city is the scene of a religious event that brings together thousands of believers and curious people?

San Gennaro, or Saint Januarius in English, is the patron saint of Naples. Legend has it that in the 4th century, despite being beheaded, a woman was able to collect his blood in two vials. These relics have since been kept in the city's cathedral. And that's where the miracle happens: the saint's normally solid blood liquefies during celebrations in his honor, three times a year.

The biggest of these celebrations takes place on September 19. Neapolitans gather in droves, praying and eagerly awaiting the moment when the blood will change its state. If the miracle happens, it's a sign of good omen for the city for the coming year.

So, if you find yourself in Naples in September, don't hesitate to immerse yourself in this unique tradition. You will witness a devotion and faith that defies centuries and skeptics.

Fact 86 - The dragons of Piedmontese legends

In the heart of the Piedmont mountains, ancient stories tell of strange creatures. Have you ever heard of the dragons that, according to legends, once inhabited this area?

The ancients say that these mountains, with their snow-capped peaks and deep valleys, were the territory of fearsome dragons. These fire-breathing beasts jealously guarded fabulous treasures, hidden in secret caves. Some daring villagers, armed with courage, have tried to seize these riches, but few have managed to outwit the vigilance of the dragons.

One of the most famous tales of Piedmont tells the story of a young shepherd who, with the help of an old witch, manages to put a dragon to sleep and seize its treasure. But instead of keeping it to himself, the shepherd uses the gold to help his village prosper.

Next time you're walking in the Piedmontese mountains, take a good look around. Who knows? Maybe the warm breath you feel on the back of your neck is that of a dragon watching over its hidden treasure.

Fact 87 - The Mystery of the Ghosts of Tuscany

Tuscany, with its gentle hills and medieval towns, is the birthplace of many stories and legends. But did you know that this region is also famous for its ghost stories and mysterious apparitions?

The narrow alleys of cities like Siena and Florence are the setting for tales dating back to the Middle Ages, where wandering spirits are spotted at nightfall. In Florence, for example, some claim to have seen the spirit of Bianca Capello, a 16th-century noblewoman, who wanders near the Palazzo Vecchio, searching for her lost love.

Then there's the Villa de Medici in Fiesole, where unseen musicians would play melancholic melodies at night. Locals talk of an interrupted wedding party that supposedly took place centuries ago, and whose guests continue to celebrate eternally.

So, on your next visit to Tuscany, if you hear a distant echo or feel an unexplained presence, remember the ancient legends. Maybe you're in the company of the ghosts of Tuscany.

Fact 88 - The Riddle of the Temples of Sicily

Did you know that Sicily, the Mediterranean island renowned for its beaches and cuisine, also hides mysterious remains that defy time? The Valley of the Temples in Agrigento is a perfect example of this.

Dating back to the ancient Greek period, this series of Doric temples spans an area of nearly 1300 hectares. These structures, like the Temple of Concord, are among the best preserved outside Greece. But what makes these temples so fascinating is their architectural enigma. While some have survived almost intact, others lie in ruins, for no apparent reason.

The Temple of Heracles, for example, has had ten of its columns rebuilt, while the rest lie on the ground. The reasons for these disparities remain a matter of debate among historians and archaeologists. Some put forward theories of natural disasters, while others believe in human destruction.

Next time you're visiting Sicily, be sure to explore these enigmatic temples. Their secrets, though silent, still whisper the stories of an ancient civilization.

Fact 89 - The Adventures of Saint Nicholas

Do you remember the tale of St. Nicholas, the generous protector of children? You might be surprised to learn that its roots go back to southern Italy, and more specifically to Bari.

Saint Nicholas, who lived in the 4th century in present-day Turkey, was renowned for his boundless generosity. After his death, his legacy lived on through legends and traditions. In the 11th century, his relics were transferred from Myra in Turkey to the Basilica of San Nicola in Bari, where they still rest today.

The story goes that a group of sailors from Bari stole these relics to save them from possible desecration during the invasions. This action established a strong bond between Saint Nicholas and the Italian city, making him the patron saint of Bari.

On your next visit to southern Italy, make a stop in Bari to feel the living presence of St. Nicholas. Its basilica is a tangible reminder of the rich and complex mix of folklore, faith, and history that intertwine in Italy.

Fact 90 - The Mysterious Bridge of Sighs

Have you ever wondered why such a beautiful bridge in Venice has a melancholic name like "Bridge of Sighs"? Despite its romantic name, the origin of this name has much darker roots.

Built in the early 17th century, this Istrian stone bridge connects the Palazzo Ducale (Doge's Palace) to the former prisons. Prisoners crossed this bridge after being tried in the palace, and before being locked up in the dark, damp cells. It is said that these convicts heaved a sigh as they passed on deck, taking a last look at the magnificent Venice through its small windows.

Although the name evokes feelings of sadness, the Bridge of Sighs is one of the most photographed sights in Venice, with its detailed white architecture.

The next time you're walking around Venice and standing in front of this bridge, take a moment to reflect on the souls who crossed it and appreciate the rich tapestry of stories and legends that envelop this fascinating city.

Fact 91 - The Wonderful Valley of the Temples

Have you ever dreamed of traveling back in time and exploring ancient Greece? In Sicily, there is a magical place that almost allows you to do just that: the Valley of the Temples. This archaeological site in Agrigento is a precious witness to the greatness of ancient Greek civilization in Italy.

Established in the sixth century B.C., this monumental complex includes the ruins of seven Doric temples. Perhaps the most impressive is the Temple of Concord, which, thanks to its restoration in the 18th century, still stands majestically, almost intact. As you walk around, you can almost hear the whispers of the ancient Sicilians who once walked on these same stones.

But the Valley is not just a collection of ancient ruins. It is a landscape where history, art and nature merge harmoniously. Olive, almond and carob trees intertwine their branches around the columns, reminding us that nature and man have coexisted for millennia.

The next time you visit Sicily, be sure to get lost in this wonderful valley, where every stone tells a story thousands of years ago.

Fact 92 - Giotto's Art of Frescoes

Did you know that the Italian Renaissance was preceded by geniuses who laid the foundations of this major artistic movement? Among them, Giotto di Bondone, often referred to simply as Giotto, revolutionized the art of fresco.

At a time when Byzantine art, with its gilded icons and stylized figures, dominated the scene, Giotto introduced a new approach. In the Upper Basilica of Assisi, his frescoes depict the life of St. Francis with an emotion and realism that had never been seen before. He brought his characters to life, giving them depth, movement, and individuality.

In the Scrovegni Chapel in Padua, his masterpiece, the emotions of the figures are revealed in their expressions, postures and interactions. These murals tell biblical stories in a way that deeply touches those who observe them, making them eternally relevant.

So, the next time you admire the works of the great masters of the Renaissance, remember Giotto. It was he who laid the first stones, leading Italy into an unprecedented artistic era.

Fact 93 - The exploits of the Lombard League

Do you remember the alliances formed to resist the invaders or to defend a common cause? The Lombard League, formed in the 12th century, is a striking example of this solidarity between Italian cities.

Faced with the rule and ambitions of the Holy Roman Emperor Frederick Barbarossa, several cities in northern Italy joined forces. Milan, Venice, Padua, Mantua, and many others, united to resist this emperor who sought to assert his power over the Lombard region.

The most symbolic moment of their resistance took place in 1176, at the Battle of Legnano. Despite their internal differences and rivalries, the cities of the Lombard League fought valiantly against the imperial forces and won a memorable victory. This triumph was immortalized in the famous Italian patriotic song "La Battaglia di Legnano".

Thanks to this spirit of unity, the Lombard League not only repelled a powerful invader, but it also left an indelible mark on Italian history, reminding us of the strength of solidarity and determination.

Fact 94 - The Charm of Tivoli Gardens

Have you ever dreamed of strolling through lush gardens, steeped in history and beauty? The Tivoli Gardens, a short distance from Rome, are exactly the kind of places that might figure in these dreams.

Since Roman times, Tivoli has been a popular destination for its thermal virtues. But what really attracts visitors today is the Villa d'Este. This Renaissance masterpiece, built in the 16th century for Cardinal Ippolito d'Este, is brimming with majestic fountains, pools, waterfalls, and shaded walkways. One of the most remarkable fountains is that of Neptune, where water gushes out in a spectacular dance.

As you walk around, you will also discover Villa Adriana, a former imperial residence dating back to the 2nd century. Its vast ruins, mixed with architectural elements from all over the Roman Empire, evoke the past greatness of Emperor Hadrian.

Let yourself be charmed by Tivoli, where every stone and every drop of water tells a story, making these gardens a true jewel of poetry and serenity.

Fact 95 - The legend of the castles of the Aosta Valley

Have you ever heard of the majestic castles nestled in Valle d'Aosta, the Alpine valley in northwestern Italy? They are not only emblematic of medieval architecture, but also carry with them fascinating legends.

The Château de Fénis, for example, is famous for its multiple towers and fortified enclosure. According to an ancient legend, its walls are home to the ghost of a white lady. She would appear on full moon nights, mourning a lost love and wandering in search of comfort.

Then there's the Château de Verrès, which stands imposingly on a rocky hill. Legend has it that a princess was imprisoned there by her own father, punished for choosing a love she disapproved of. The murmurs of his melancholy songs would still echo through the vaulted halls.

Don't forget to visit these castles during your stay in Italy. Not only for their architectural splendor, but also for immersing you in the mysteries and stories that surround them. They are living proof that history and folklore can coexist harmoniously.

Fact 96 - The Miracles of Monte Sant'Angelo

Have you ever heard of Monte Sant'Angelo in Italy? It is a sacred mountain located in Puglia, and it is famous for the many miracles associated with it.

For centuries, pilgrims from all over the world have climbed this mountain to get to the Archangel Michael, who is said to have appeared in this place in the 5th century. According to legend, he appeared in a cave, leaving an imprint of his foot on the stone. Today, this cave has become a shrine dedicated to the archangel.

Many testimonies report miraculous healings on this sacred mountain. People suffering from incurable illnesses or disabilities have regained their health after praying at this shrine. These stories strengthened the faith of many pilgrims and made this place even more special.

Next time you visit Italy, don't miss the opportunity to visit Monte Sant'Angelo. Whether you are a believer or simply curious, this place steeped in history and mystery will undoubtedly fascinate you.

Fact 97 - The Secret History of Panettone

Do you know the history of Panettone, the Italian brioche topped with candied fruit and raisins? Although it is now a staple of the holiday season in Italy, its origins remain shrouded in mystery.

One of the most popular legends tells the story of a Milanese nobleman, Ugo degli Atellani, who fell in love with the daughter of a baker named Toni. To impress the young woman's father, Ugo is said to have invented a soft and tall brioche, which he named "Pan de Toni", which in time became "Panettone".

Another version relates that at the court of Duke Ludovico Sforza, during a Christmas meal, the planned dessert was accidentally burned. It was a simple kitchen helper, Toni, who saved the evening with his personal brioche recipe. She was so beloved that she was nicknamed in her honor.

Whatever its true origin, Panettone is now synonymous with celebration and sharing in Italy. When you bite into this delicious brioche, remember the legends surrounding it, adding a touch of magic to every bite.

Fact 98 - The Magic of Venice's Palaces

Have you ever walked along the canals of Venice, marveling at the splendor of the palaces shimmering in the water? These buildings, symbols of the Serenissima's glorious past, tell centuries of history, intrigue and romance.

One of the most famous is the Palazzo Ducale, once the residence of the Doges of Venice. Its Gothic façade and opulent halls are a testament to the power and wealth of the Republic of Venice at its height. Imagine walking through its corridors, where important political decisions were made and state secrets whispered.

Then there's the Palazzo Ca' d'Oro, a masterpiece of Venetian architecture, with its pink and white marble details. It was once the home of the powerful Contarini family, who hosted lavish parties, attracting nobles from all over Europe.

Each palace in Venice has its own story to tell, its own secrets whispered in the ornate halls. On your next visit to Venice, take a moment to lose yourself in these tales and let yourself be transported by the magic of the Venetian palaces.

Fact 99 - The Fairy Tale of Lake Garda

Have you ever heard of Lake Garda, that serene stretch of water nestled in the middle of the mountains of northern Italy? This lake, the largest in the country, is surrounded by legends and fairy tales that have amazed young and old alike for generations.

One of these stories tells that in the past, nymphs inhabited the clear waters of the lake. These creatures, endowed with ethereal beauty, danced under the moonbeams, creating a melody so sweet that even the fish stopped to listen.

It is also said that a sunken castle lies deep in the lake. This castle, once inhabited by a pure-hearted princess, was submerged on a stormy night. Some say that on clear nights, you can still see the lights of the castle shining from the depths.

The next time you're standing on the shores of Lake Garda, close your eyes and imagine the stories these waters have to tell. Maybe you'll feel the magic of the fairy tales that have rocked so many generations.

Fact 100 - The Naval Battles of Lake Bolsena

Have you ever wondered if a lake could be the scene of naval battles? Lake Bolsena in central Italy has a history as deep as its waters. Located in the Lazio region, this lake is surrounded by myths and historical narratives that give it a mystical aura.

In the Middle Ages, rivalries between neighboring city-states turned this tranquil lake into a naval battlefield. Entire fleets, made up of small craft adapted to inland waters, faced each other in epic battles, where strategic advantage constantly changed hands.

A notable example is the battle of 1275, where the city of Orvieto challenged the city of Viterbo for control of the lake's resources. Chronicles of the time describe an intense battle, with bows firing from all sides and boats engaged in daring manoeuvres.

Today, the tranquil waters of Lake Bolsena hide the secrets of these historic battles. The next time you wander its shores, remember the naval battles that once stirred its waters and shaped the region's history.

Conclusion

And there you have it, dear reader, our journey through the hidden wonders of Italy is coming to an end. From north to south, from east to west, we have explored together stories, legends and facts that make this country a priceless treasure trove of culture and history.

As you read through these pages, you may have felt wonder, surprise, or astonishment. Maybe you've even been inspired to visit some of these mystical places or learn more about the legendary figures we've discovered together.

But beyond these facts and anecdotes, Italy, with its rich and vibrant past, reminds us that every stone, every street, every building has a story to tell. That's the beauty of adventure: realizing that behind every corner is a story waiting to be discovered.

I hope that this book has given you a new insight into Italy, and that these stories will accompany you on your next escapades or simply in your daydreams. Always keep this curiosity inside you, because every destination has its secrets. Arrivederci, and may your future travels have a thousand and one more discoveries in store for you!

Marc Dresgui

Quiz

1) In which Italian region is there a rich tradition of fairy tales?

    a) Tuscany

    b) Aosta Valley

    c) Sicily

    d) Lombardy

2) What gemstone are the caves of Carrara famous for?

    a) Granite

    b) Jade

    c) Marble

    d) Sapphire

3) Which holiday in Naples celebrates a miraculous event involving blood?

    a) Feast of San Marco

    b) Feast of San Pietro

    c) Feast of San Gennaro

    d) Feast of San Francesco

4) What region do dragon legends come from?

    a) Sardinia

    b) Veneto

c) Piedmont

d) Calabria

5) In which Italian region do you often hear ghost stories?

a) Abruzzi

b) Tuscany

c) Basilicata

d) Marches

6) Which island is famous for its ancient temples?

a) Sardinia

b) Elbe

c) Capri

d) Sicily

7) Which famous bridge in Venice has often been associated with tales of sadness?

a) Ponte della Libertà

b) Ponte di Rialto

c) Ponte dei Sospiri

d) Ponte dell'Accademia

8) Which city is associated with the legend of Santa Claus, Saint Nicholas?

a) Florence
b) Kite
c) Bari
d) Turin

9) In which region is there a valley filled with ancient Greek temples?

a) Arno Valley
b) Valley of the Temples
c) Susa Valley
d) Isonzo Valley

10) In what sacred place in Italy are miracles said to occur?

a) Monte Sant'Angelo
b) Mount Vesuvius
c) Mount Etna
d) Monte Rosa

11) What delicious Italian pastry is often associated with Christmas?

a) Cannoli
b) Tiramisu

c) Panettone

d) Panna Cotta

12) Where can you admire sumptuous palaces that seem to float on water?

a) Naples

b) Venice

c) Genoa

d) Trieste

13) Which famous Italian lake is often surrounded by magical tales?

a) Lake maggiore

b) Lake Garda

c) Lake Iseo

d) Lake Orta

14) On which Italian lake did ancient naval battles take place?

a) Lake Bolsena

b) Lake Como

c) Lake Trasimeno

d) Lake Vico

15) In which region of Italy can you discover castles full of legends?

a) Campania
b) Emilia-Romagna
c) Valle d'Aosta
d) Umbria

16) Which artist is famous for his revolutionary frescoes in Italy?

a) Da Vinci
b) Giotto
c) Botticelli
d) Caravaggio

17) Which historical alliance played a key role in the fight against the Holy Roman Emperors?

a) Tyrrhenian Alliance
b) Lombard League
c) Adriatic Coalition
d) Union Siculo

18) In which Italian city can you explore beautiful ancient gardens, full of history?

a) Naples
b) Tivoli

c) Palermo

d) Mantua

19) Which architectural building in Rome is famous for its central oculus?

a) Colosseum

b) Pantheon

c) Roman Forum

d) Castel Sant'Angelo

20) Which town in the Puglia region is famous for its cave dwellings?

a) Bologna

b) Matera

c) Lecce

d) Taranto

Answers

1) In which Italian region is there a rich tradition of fairy tales?

Correct answer: b) Aosta Valley

2) What gemstone are the caves of Carrara famous for?

Correct answer: c)Marble

3) Which holiday in Naples celebrates a miraculous event involving blood?

Correct answer: c) Feast of San Gennaro

4) What region do dragon legends come from?

Correct answer: c)Piedmont

5) In which Italian region do you often hear ghost stories?

Correct answer: b)Tuscany

6) Which island is famous for its ancient temples?

Correct answer: d)Sicily

7) Which famous bridge in Venice has often been associated with tales of sadness?

Correct answer: c)Ponte dei Sospiri

8) Which city is associated with the legend of Santa Claus, Saint Nicholas?

Correct answer: c)Bari

9) In which region is there a valley filled with ancient Greek temples?

Correct answer: b) Valley of the Temples

10) In what sacred place in Italy are miracles said to occur?

Correct answer: a) Monte Sant'Angelo

11) What delicious Italian pastry is often associated with Christmas?

Correct answer: c)Panettone

12) Where can you admire sumptuous palaces that seem to float on water?

Correct answer: b)Venice

13) Which famous Italian lake is often surrounded by magical tales?

Correct answer: b)Lake Garda

14) On which Italian lake did ancient naval battles take place?

Correct answer: a)Lake Bolsena

15) In which region of Italy can you discover castles full of legends?

Correct answer: c)Valle d'Aosta

16) Which artist is famous for his revolutionary frescoes in Italy?

Correct answer: b) Giotto

17) Which historical alliance played a key role in the fight against the Holy Roman Emperors?

Correct answer: b) Lombard League

18) In which Italian city can you explore beautiful ancient gardens, full of history?

Correct answer: b) Tivoli

19) Which architectural building in Rome is famous for its central oculus?

Correct answer: b) Pantheon

20) Which town in the Puglia region is famous for its cave dwellings?

Correct answer: b) Matera

Made in United States
Troutdale, OR
10/20/2024

23944794R00066